WOMEN & GOD
DROPS IN THE SEA OF TIME

Translated & Edited by John Gallas

SLG
Press

© 2022 SLG Press
First Edition 2022
Contemplative Poetry 5

Print ISBN 978-0-7283-0325-6
Contemplative Poetry Series ISBN 978-0-7283-0319-5

John Gallas asserts his right under the Copyright, Designs and Patents Act 1988, to be identified as the translator of: 'Two Little Words', 'Why are you groping like somebody blind', 'Sometimes they Kiss', 'False Modesty', 'Credo', 'How will you manage', 'I stopped my travels', 'At Lake Balaton', 'Tell your beads', 'Beyond a hundred thousand miles of night', 'Sonnet', 'Considering the Greatness of Love', 'Ever lofty, ever green', 'A Christian Sonnet', 'World! Why do you hound me so?', 'Beauty's Fragile Light', 'My house was built for two', 'Sleepsong', 'The Pillow', 'The Crucifixion', 'When He died of thirst', I am a fountain', 'The Easter Holiday', 'Spring Song', 'Procession of Our Lady of the Ship', 'My life's small ship', 'The Ox', 'Prayer for a Sound Sleep', 'Night', 'Prayer', 'More than Love', 'On a Butterfly', 'I am weary now', 'Big Wide World', 'And when night comes on', 'My new white dress', 'The Waiting Pinetree', 'The Volcano Flower', 'Morning', 'We Die like Tomorrow', 'Lullaby', 'Her Prayer', 'Resignation', 'At a Graveside', 'Visitors', 'Psalm', 'Hymn', 'Twelve Epigrams', 'Render alms'.

Edited, designed and typeset in Bembo by Julia Craig-McFeely

SLG Press
Convent of the Incarnation
Fairacres • Oxford
www.slgpress.co.uk

Printed by
Grosvenor Group Ltd, Loughton, Essex

Contents

Author Biographies   iv

About John Gallas   xvi

⤙⤚

Two Little Words (St Teresa of Ávila)   1

I am not skilled to understand (Dora Greenwell)   2

My Vocation (Toru Dutt)   3

Why are you groping like somebody blind (Lalleshwari)   3

Sometimes they kiss (St Catherine of Siena)   4

False Modesty (Akka Mahadevi)   5

How will you manage (Princess Ōku)   5

Credo (Gabriela Mistral)   6

I stopped my travels (Mirabai)   7

The Best Thing in the World (Elizabeth Barrett Browning)   8

At Lake Balaton (Atala Kisfaludy)   9

A Prayer for Mr T. W., Who was then in the West Indies (Jane Cave)   10

In the Forest (Sarojini Naidu)   11

Tell your beads (Gangasati)   12

Sonnet (Vittoria Colonna)   13

Be still, my soul (Catharina Amalia Dorothea von Schlegel)   14

Beyond a hundred thousand miles of night (St Frances of Rome)   15

Considering the Greatness of Love (Hadwijch of Brabant)   16

O God, from Thee we would not stray (Lucy Larcom)   19

Dandelions (Frances Ellen Watkins Harper)   20

I never saw a moor (Emily Dickinson)   21

Ever lofty, ever green (Hildegard von Bingen)   22

A Christian Sonnet (Madeleine de l'Aubespine)   23

World! Why do you hound me so? (Juana Inés de la Cruz)   24

Beauty's Fragile Light (Hedvig Charlotta Nordenflycht)   25

My house was built for two (Anonymous, Japan) — 25

A Christmas Carol, or Verses on the Nativity of Christ (Anne Ley) — 26

Sleepsong (Anonymous, The Gambia) — 27

The Pillow (St Thérèse of Lisieux) — 28

Christ, the Nazarene (Constance Naden) — 29

The Crucifixion (Elizaveta Dmitrieva) — 30

When He died of thirst (Elizaveta Dmitrieva) — 31

I am a fountain (Zeynep Hatun) — 31

The Easter Holiday (Louise Otto-Peters) — 32

Spring Song (Catharina Regina von Greiffenberg) — 33

Procession of Our Lady of the Ship (Rosalia de Castro) — 34

My life's small ship (St Faustina of Poland) — 35

On Death (Anne Killigrew) — 36

The Ox (Anonymous, Yemen) — 38

Composed During a Thunder-storm (Judith Lomax) — 39

Prayer for a Sound Sleep (St Gertrude of Nivelles) — 40

For Deliverance from a Fever (Anne Bradstreet) — 41

To a Gentleman and Lady on the Death of the Lady's Brother and Sister, and a Child of the Name Avis, Aged One Year (Phillis Wheatley) — 42

Night (Rabia al-Basri) — 44

Prayer (Rabia al-Basri) — 44

More than Love (Anonymous, Jordan) — 45

Indian Love-Song (Sarojini Naidu) — 46

On a Butterfly (Gertrudis Gomez de Alvellaneda) — 46

I am weary now (Luise Hensel) — 47

Big Wide World (Veronica Micle) — 48

And when night comes on (St Edith Stein) — 49

My new white dress (Anonymous, Equatorial Guinea) — 50

The One Certainty (Christina Rossetti) — 51

Oh, what a lantern (Mary Sidney Herbert) — 52

Sonnet written on the Eve of her Execution (Mary Stuart) — 53

The Waiting Pinetree (Habba Khatoun) — 54

The Volcano Flower (Amable Tastu) — 55

We Die like Tomorrow (Magda Isanos) — 56

Lullaby (Anonymous, Myanmar) — 57

Morning (Maria Brunamonti) — 58

Her Prayer (St Agatha) — 58

Resignation (Brigida Agüero)   59
At a Graveside (Anna Maria Lenngren)   60
Visitors (Anonymous, Rwanda)   61
Psalm (Anna Jonassen)   62
Hymn (St Kassia of Constantinople)   63
Twelve Epigrams (St Kassia of Constantinople)   64
Render Alms (Avvaiyar)   66

Index of first lines   68
Index of authors   71

AUTHOR BIOGRAPHIES

St Agatha (231–251) was born in Catania, part of the Roman Province of Sicily, and is one of several virgin martyrs who are commemorated by name in the Canon of the Mass. Agatha was put to death during the Decian persecution (250–253) in Catania, for her determined profession of faith, and is one of the most highly venerated virgin martyrs of Christian antiquity. (58)

Brigida Agüero (1837–1866) was the daughter of the distinguished Cuban poet Francisco Agüero y Estrada and Ana Maria Agüero y Varona. She grew up on the family farm where she was initially tutored by her parents but later attended a school and began to release her poems. After attending an academy run by the Camagüey Philharmonic Society, she was appointed a faculty member in recognition of her talents. (59)

Madeleine de l'Aubespine (1546–1596) was a French aristocrat, lady-in-waiting to Catherine de Medicis, poet, and literary patron. She was one of the only female poets praised by Pierre de Ronsard. L'Aubespine was a patron of the elite literary circles of sixteenth-century France, where she was widely influential. She was responsible for translating works from other languages into the French vernacular. (23)

Avvaiyar (*c.* 3rd century BC) was the title of more than one female poet active during different periods of Tamil literature. The name translates literally as 'Respectable Woman'. These were some of the most famous and important female poets of the Tamil canon. The first Avvaiyar lived during the Sangam period and wrote 59 poems in the classical Tamil poetic work, the *Puṟanāṉūṟu*. (66)

Anne Bradstreet (1612–1672) was a Puritan and the first published English poet in North America. She is notable for her large corpus of poetry, as well as personal writings. Her works tend to be directed to members of her family and are hopeful and positive in tone despite her having led a difficult life. Her faith supported her positive outlook and the strength of character that is evident in her writing. (41)

Elizabeth Barrett Browning (1806–1861) was an English poet. Her volume *Poems* (1844) was highly regarded and led to her meeting and marrying the poet Robert Browning. She spent the latter years of her life in Italy, dying in Florence. Her work had a major influence on prominent writers of the day, including the American poets Edgar Allan Poe and Emily Dickinson. (8)

Maria Brunamonti (1841–1903) was an Italian poet and scholar. Her poetry dealt with contemporary issues, and she became the first woman in Italy to vote, due to the high regard in which her political poetry was held. In her works she explored conflicts, such as the 1859 Perugia uprising, the Battle of Magenta and the Battle of Solferino. She was a devout Catholic and dedicated some of her works to Pope Pius IX. (58)

Rosalia de Castro (1837–1885) was a Galician poet who strongly identified with her native Galicia and the celebration of the Galician language. She was well-educated and expected to speak and write in Spanish, but she wrote her early poems in Galician, a dialect considered by the educated as 'illiterate and churlish'. Her defiant gesture won her the love and admiration of the less-educated populace. (34)

St Catherine of Siena (1347–1380) was a lay member of the Dominican Order, and a mystic, activist, and author. She was influential in Italian literature and also within the Catholic Church and Italian politics. She was instrumental in restoring the papacy to Rome, and in brokering peace in conflicts between Italian city states. She was proclaimed a Doctor of the Church in 1970, meaning that her writings have special authority in Roman Catholicism. (4)

Jane Cave (1754–1812) was a Welsh poet who educated herself by reading books and poetry. She wrote in English and moved around England during her lifetime. She is particularly known for her poetry on religious subjects. She belonged to the Countess of Huntingdon's Connexion (a group of Evangelical churches associated with the Calvinistic Methodist movement) but was also known to attend Anglican churches. (10)

Vittoria Colonna (1492–1547) was an educated, married noblewoman whose husband was in captivity in France. When her husband died she joined a convent in Rome but did not take vows. She developed relationships within the intellectual circles of Ischia and Naples and became one of the most popular female poets of sixteenth-century Italy. She is known to have been a muse to Michelangelo Buonarroti. (13)

Juana Inés de la Cruz OSH (Juana Ramírez de Asbaje, 1648–1695) was a proto-feminist Mexican writer, philosopher, composer and poet. She was almost entirely self-taught and became a Hieronymite nun whose life and teaching created a focal point for Spain's female intellectual elite. After centuries of neglect she is now considered by some to be the most accomplished author of the Spanish Americas. (24)

Emily Dickinson (1830–1886) was an American poet. She was relatively unknown during her lifetime but is now considered to be one of the most important figures in American poetry. Although a prolific writer, only ten of her nearly 1,800 poems were published in her lifetime. Many of her poems deal with themes of death and immortality and also explore aesthetics, society, nature and spirituality. (21)

Elisaveta Dmitrieva (Cherubina de Gabriak, 1887–1928) was a Russian poet who had been crippled by tuberculosis of the bones. She was exiled to Tashkent in 1927 in relation to her membership of the Anthroposophic Society. Shortly before her death, she wrote a set of poems under the pseudonym Li Xiang Zi, a fictional Chinese poet exiled for his belief in the immortality of human spirit. (30–1)

Toru Dutt (1856–1877) was a Bengali translator and poet from British India, who wrote in English and French. She came from a liberal family where education, art and linguistics were encouraged and is one of the founding figures of Indo-Anglian literature. She is known for her volumes of poetry in English and for a novel in French. Her poems explore themes of loneliness, longing, patriotism and nostalgia. (3)

St Faustina of Poland (1905–1938) was a Polish Roman Catholic nun and mystic. Throughout her life she reported having visions of Jesus and conversations with Him, which she noted in her diary. She entered the Congregation of the Sisters of Our Lady of Mercy in 1925 where, carefully observing the rules of religious life, externally nothing revealed her rich mystical interior life. She is now venerated as the Apostle of Divine Mercy. (35)

St Frances of Rome (1384–1440) is an Italian saint who was a wife, mother, mystic, organizer of charitable services, and a Benedictine oblate. Throughout her life she struggled with an internal conflict between her married state and the desire for religious life. She founded a community of secular religious, the Olivetan Oblates of the Virgin Mary, who share a life of prayer and service. (15)

Gangasati (Gangabai Gohil, 13th century) was a medieval devotional poet and saint from the Bhakti movement of western India. She and her husband were devout and their home became a centre of religious activity. She composed fifty-two devotional songs (*bhajans*) in the Gujarati language exploring the path of devotion. Notably they do not mention any traditional Hindu deity but address God in general, without any form or attributes, and reflect different ways of attaining spiritual peace. (12)

St Gertrude of Nivelles (626–659) was a noblewoman who refused to marry. When her father died she and her mother moved to Nivelles in Belgium, where they founded an Abbey in which Gertrude eventually became abbess. She was known for her devotion to scholarly and charitable works, and experienced spiritual visions, but her ascetic lifestyle, which included long periods without food or sleep, led to her early death. (40)

Gertrudis Gomez de Alvellaneda (1814–1873) was a Cuban-born Spanish writer. Her family moved to Spain in 1836, where she started writing under the soubriquet La Peregrina (The Pilgrim). She returned to Cuba in 1859, returning to Spain after the death of her husband in 1863. She was a prolific writer of plays and poetry, but her most famous work is the anti-slavery novel *Sab*, published in Madrid in 1841. (46)

Dora Greenwell (1821–1882) was an English poet, considered a writer of rare spiritual insight and fine poetic genius, who was generally believed to be a member of the Society of Friends. She was often compared to Christina Rossetti. In addition to poetry, she was an accomplished essayist on spiritual and social issues. She was a champion of women's education and suffrage and a vociferous opponent of the slave trade. (2)

Catharina Regina von Greiffenberg (1633–1694) was an Austrian poet from a noble family, and one of the most significant German-language female writers of the early modern period. Her work is often profoundly personal and expressed as an internal monologue focusing on the nature of the relationship between the believer and God. It is marked by a mystical use of imagery, as well as linguistic inventiveness. (33)

Hadewijch of Brabant (1200–1248) was a poet and known as a 'minnemystik', a mystic who is centered on 'minne' or love, a form that appears to have originated with St Bernard. Her writings include descriptions of visions, prose letters and poetry, and she often used courtly love images in her visionary writings and appear to have been addressed to a community of Beguines, where it is believed she lived and held a position of influence. (16–18)

Frances Ellen Watkins Harper (1825-1911) was an American abolitionist, suffragist, poet, teacher, public speaker, and writer. She was one of the first African-American women to be published in the United States and had a long and prolific career, publishing commercially-successful poetry and prose, including anti-slavery literature. She made history as the first black woman to publish a short story and was among the first to publish a full novel. (20–1)

Zeynep Hatun (1420–1474) was one of the first significant female voices of Ottoman poetry and is the first known female poet of Divan literature. She was the daughter of a judge in Amasya, and a contemporary of the poetess Mihri Hatun. Very little is known of her life apart from mentions in the work of other poets, who agree that she lived in Istanbul. (31)

Luise Hensel (1798–1876) was a German teacher and religious poet. She was the daughter of a Lutheran minister and showed unusual talent for writing from an early age. One of her pupils, Clara Fey, was to become the founder of the Sisters of the Poor Children of Jesus. She lived a secular life as a virgin and spent her last years living in a convent. Her published poetry shows a moving and wistful piety common to German religious poetry of the era. (47)

Mary Sidney Herbert (1561–1621) was one of the first English women to gain a significant reputation for her poetry and her literary patronage. John Bodenham, in his verse miscellany *Belvidere, or the Garden of the Muses* (1600), listed her alongside Philip Sidney (her brother), Edmund Spenser and William Shakespeare as one of the notable authors of the day. She was known above all for her lyrical translation of the Psalms. (52)

Hildegard von Bingen (1098–1179) also known as St Hildegard and the 'Sibyl of the Rhine', was a highly educated German Benedictine abbess who was a philosopher, mystic and visionary. She also practiced medicine. She was a prolific writer of music and poetry, as well as theological, botanical, and medicinal works, and is widely considered to be the founder of scientific natural history in Germany. She was proclaimed a Doctor of the Church in 2012. (22)

Magda Isanos (1916–1944) was a Romanian poet. Her parents were doctors at a psychiatric hospital. Initially she studied law, and while at university became attached to left-wing student societies. After graduating, she worked briefly as a lawyer and became active in the literary circle that encompassed visionary artists of the time, including her future husband, the writer Eusebiu Camilar. Her lyric poems hover between despair and euphoria. (56)

Anna Jonassen (1871–1939) was a Norwegian hymn writer who worked as a telegraph operator in Stavanger and was active in the Norwegian Mission Society, which is headquartered in the city. She wrote a number of religious songs, one of which, the childrens' song 'I am small, but I want to', is included in the current Norwegian Hymn Book. (62)

St Kassia of Constantinople (810–865) was a Byzantine-Greek composer, hymnographer and poet. She is the only known woman whose music appears in the Byzantine liturgy. Approximately fifty of her hymns survive, most of which are *sticheron* (a hymn that is sung during the morning and evening service of churches which follow the Byzantine Rite), though the attribution for at least half of those is uncertain. (63–5)

Habba Khatoun (1554–1609) was a Kashmiri Muslim poet and ascetic who composed songs in Kashmiri. She was the wife of Yousuf Shah Chak, the last Emperor of Kashmir. Her songs, widely popular across Kashmir, are frequently mournful and full of the sorrow of separation. She has a profound presence in the oral tradition and is hailed as the last independent poet-queen of Kashmir. (4)

Anne Killigrew (1660–1685) was an English poet and painter, described by contemporaries as 'a Grace for beauty', and 'a Muse for wit'. She and her family were active in literary and court circles in London and her poems were circulated in manuscript. They have been published several times by modern scholars. Dryden compared Killigrew's poetic abilities to the Greek poet of antiquity, Sappho. (36–7)

Atala Kisfaludy (1836–1911) was a Hungarian poet from a noble family. She was the first woman to be a member of the Petőfi Society, a Hungarian literary society up to 1944. She was part of the cultural life of the southwestern Hungarian city of Kaposvár and began to write poetry during an illness in 1858. In 1861, she founded and edited a childrens' magazine with the children's writer Richard Szabó. (9)

Lalleshwari (*c.* 1320–1392) also known as Lalla Ded, was a Kashmiri mystic of the Kashmir Shaivism school of Hindu philosophy. She composed four-line mystic poems called *vakh*, which means 'speech' in Kashmiri. She wrote in the local vernacular, which made Shaivite teachings that had previously been available only in Sanskrit, available to all Kashmiris. (3)

Lucy Larcom (1824–1893) was an American teacher, abolitionist, poet, and author. She began working in a textile mill at the age of eleven. Some of her earliest published works were unsigned, and one was attributed to Emerson. She also wrote patriotic lyrics that attracted considerable attention during the American Civil War. Much of her writing was on religious themes and embodied her beliefs on matters concerning the spiritual life. (19)

Anna Maria Lenngren (1754–1817) was one of the most famous poets in Swedish history. Although her first poems were written in an ecstatic and passionate manner common in the religious circles of her father, her later work took on a sardonic satirical style. Her defence of the right of women to participate in intellectual work is particularly evident in the forewords to her publications. She is one of the few eighteenth-century Swedish poets who are still commonly read and published. (60)

Anne Ley (1599–1641) was an English writer, teacher, and polemicist. She was married to Roger Ley, a writer and a curate of St Leonard's Church in Shoreditch, who shared her ardent royalist and religious conformist sentiments. Her poems and other pious writings were written in her commonplace book (c. 1620–1641), to which her husband added his own works after her death. (26)

Judith Lomax (1774–1828) was an American poet and religious writer and the first woman in Virginia to publish a single-author volume of poetry. Her personal faith mixed elements of the Anglican, Methodist and Baptist traditions. She was instrumental in the rejuvenation of the Episcopal Church in Virginia after the American Revolutionary War. She viewed her writing as an important way to practice her faith and a tool of evangelization. (39)

Akka Mahadevi (c. 1130–1160) was one of the early female poets writing in Kannada dialect, and was highly regarded in the Lingayatism sect of Hinduism in the twelfth century. The term Akka ('elder Sister') is an honorific given to great Lingayat saints and an indication of the high regard in which she is held. She composed some 430 *Vachana* poems (a form of spontaneous mystical poems) and several short devotional essays. (5)

Veronica Micle (Ana Câmpeanu, 1850–1889) was a Romanian poet, author and translator. Her first poem was inspired by Dante's life. She had a long-running love affair with the important Romanian writer Mihai Eminescu, who met her while attending her literary salon and whose style influenced her own. After his death she retired to Varatec Monastery where she compiled a volume entitled *Love and Poetry*, before taking her own life in despair. (48)

Mirabai (c. 1498–c. 1547) was a Hindu mystic poet and devotee of Krishna, also known as Meera and venerated as a Bhakti saint, particularly in the North Indian Hindu tradition. She was born into a Rajput royal family in Kudki and was known for her songs of devotion to Krishna, and for dedicating her life to worship. Like many in the Bhakti movement, she ignored gender, class, caste, and religious boundaries, and spent time caring for the poor. (7)

Gabriela Mistral (1889–1957) is the pseudonym of Lucila Godoy Alcayaga. She was a Chilean poet-diplomat, educator and humanist and in 1945 became the first Latin American author to receive a Nobel Prize in Literature. Her poetry explores the formation of Latin American identity from Native American and European influences, and includes themes of Christian faith, love and sorrow. She was a lay member of the Franciscan order. (6–7)

Constance Naden (1858–1889) was an English writer, poet and philosopher. She published two volumes of poetry, and studied, wrote and lectured on philosophy and science. She was considered by her contemporaries to be one of the nineteenth century's foremost female poets. Her poetic corpus is extremely diverse with subject matter spanning the natural world, religious faith and doubt, and philosophical ideas. (29)

Sarojini Naidu (1879–1949) was born into a middle-class family of well-educated Brahmins who sent her to London and Cambridge for her education. She was an Indian civil rights and women's emancipation activist who promoted Hindu-Muslim unity and was an important figure in India's struggle for independence. Because of the colour, imagery and lyrical quality of her poetry, Ghandi called her 'The Nightingale of India'. (11, 46)

Hedvig Charlotta Nordenflycht (1718–1763) was a Swedish poet, feminist and salon hostess. She is known for describing the existential conflict between religion and science during the age of enlightenment, and for her depiction of human love and sorrow. Known as sensitive and emotional, she was also practical, logical and strong willed when it came to defending her own literary position and the intellectual capacity of women. (25)

Princess Ōku (661–702) was a Japanese princess during the Asuka period. She was the daughter of Emperor Tenmu and witnessed the Jinshin War (672) as a young child. According to the Man'yōshū (*The Anthology of Ten Thousand Leaves*) she became the first unmarried Imperial princess to serve at the Shinto Ise Grand Shrine, which many only be entered by members of the Japanese imperial family. (5)

Louise Otto-Peters (1819–1895) was a German suffragist and women's rights movement activist who wrote novels, poetry, essays, and libretti. She started two newspapers specifically for women, and founded the *Allgemeiner Deutscher Frauenverein*. She campaigned throughout her life for better working conditions for poor women and her peers gave her the soubriquet 'Songbird of the German Women's Movement'. (32)

Rabia al-Basri (Rabia al-Adawiyya, 717–801) was a Sufi mystic and the first female Sufi Saint of Islam. She was born into extreme poverty and sold into slavery, but when famine overtook Basra she was freed and went into the desert to pray, becoming an ascetic and living a life of semi-seclusion. She made one of the greatest contributions towards the development of Sufism and was known for her pure, unconditional love of God. (44)

Christina Rossetti (1830–1894) was an English writer of romantic, devotional and children's poetry whose strong religious beliefs marked her out from the majority of other Pre-Raphaelites. Her sister became an Anglican nun in 1873, and Christina worked with the sisterhood for some time. Rossetti's works were widely praised by critics and her contemporaries, who considered her the foremost female poet of the day. (51)

Catharina Amalia Dorothea von Schlegel (1697–1768) was a German hymn writer associated with a Lutheran *Damenstift* (a convent-like secular community for unmarried Protestant women) in Cöthen. She was shaped by a renewal movement in the church known as Pietism. She corresponded with the Lutheran Biblical scholar August Hermann Francke and wrote a number of hymns in the spirit of early Pietism. (14–15)

St Edith Stein (Sr Teresa Benedicta of the Cross, 1891–1942) was a German Jewish philosopher who converted to Christianity and became a Discalced Carmelite nun. A pivotal moment in her conversion was the discovery of the works of St Teresa of Ávila. She was part of a group of 987 people deported to Auschwitz concentration camp in 1942, where she was subsequently executed in a gas chamber. She is a martyr and saint of the Catholic Church. (49)

Mary Stuart (1542–1587) was queen of Scotland from 14 December 1542 until her forced abdication in 1567. She was a devout Catholic and was beheaded in 1587 for planning to overthrow the Protestant Queen Elizabeth. Thirty-nine poems and fragments have been attributed to her, but the most interesting were the fourteen poems and fragments written in the margins of her Book of Hours, of which there is no modern edition. (53)

Amable Tastu (Sabine Casimire Amable Voïart, 1795–1885) was a French poet and writer. Although raised in a wealthy family, her parents and husband were financially ruined after the revolution of 1830, and she lived much of her life in relative poverty. Despite being widely celebrated, Tastu remained diffident about her talents. She embedded social critique in her verse which mirrored wider cultural and political currents. (55)

St Teresa of Ávila (1515–1582) was a Spanish noblewoman who became a Carmelite nun and mystic. She reformed the Carmelite Orders and was a prominent author and theologian. She was proclaimed a Doctor of the Church in 1970 and holds a special place in the lives of all Carmelites. She wrote many poems reflecting the divine visions she experienced which gave her an inner joy and peace during a period of illness and intense pain. (1)

St Thérèse of Lisieux (1873–1897), known as 'the Little Flower', was a French Discalced Carmelite nun of the cloistered community of Lisieux, Normandy. She is widely venerated and has been an influential model of sanctity because of her humility and the simplicity and practicality of her approach to the spiritual life. Her writings espouse the belief that anyone can achieve holiness by doing all things for love of God. She was proclaimed a Doctor of the Church in 1997. (28)

Phillis Wheatley (1753–1784) was the first African-American author of a published book of poetry. Born in West Africa, she was sold into slavery at the age of seven or eight and transported to North America, where she was bought by the Wheatley family of Boston. After she learned to read and write, they encouraged her poetry when they saw her talent. The London publication of her *Poems on Various Subjects, Religious and Moral* in 1773 brought her fame both in England and America, and she was emancipated shortly after. She died, however, in poverty and obscurity. (42–3)

Julia Craig-McFeely

About John Gallas

John Edward Gallas FEA (born 11 January 1950) is an Aotearoan poet. He won the International Welsh Poetry Competition in 2009 and his poem 'Cat' was *The Guardian* 'Poem of the Week' in December 2014. In 2016 he was the joint Winner of the Indigo Dreams Pamphlet Prize and was the Orkney St Magnus International Festival Poet. He has also held the positions of John Clare 'The Visit' Poet (2019) and Sutton Hoo Saxon Ship Poet (2020). In 2022 he was awarded the National Poetry Library's Brian Dempsey Memorial Poetry Prize.

Gallas was born in Wellington, Aotearoa and attended the University of Otago. He won a Commonwealth Scholarship to Merton College, Oxford to study Medieval English Literature and Old Icelandic and has since lived and worked in York, Liverpool and various other locations (presently Markfield, Leicestershire), as a bottlewasher, archaeologist and teacher. Gallas is the librettist for David Knotts' Cantata *Toads on a Tapestry*, and for Alasdair Nicolson's opera *The Iris Murders*. He has published twenty-four collections of poetry, including six anthologies and three collections of translations.

He is a Fellow of the English Association and describes himself as a biker, tramper, Leicester City football fan and quiet herbalist. A full list of his publications can be found on his website: www.johngallaspoetry.co.uk.

WOMEN & GOD
Drops in the Sea of Time

Two Little Words

Two little words from Him were enough
to change my life forever:
Love me.
What terrible labours I imagined,
what crosses to bear, as he had borne.

But Love said, *I am a song:*
if you ask me, I will sing it.
And from every brick of every house
in every street the laughter flew,
and out of every inch of sky
that dawned beyond a night of prayer:

and all my life was changed forever
by two little words from Him:
Love me.

St Teresa of Ávila (1515–1582)

I am not skilled to understand

I am not skilled to understand
What God hath willed, what God hath planned;
I only know that at His right hand
Is One Who is my Saviour!

I take Him at His word indeed;
"Christ died for sinners"—this I read;
For in my heart I find a need
Of Him to be my Saviour!

That He should leave His place on high
And come for sinful man to die,
You count it strange? So once did I,
Before I knew my Saviour!

And oh, that He fulfilled may see
The travail of His soul in me,
And with His work contented be,
As I with my dear Saviour!

Yea, living, dying, let me bring
My strength, my solace from this Spring;
That He Who lives to be my King
Once died to be my Saviour!

Dora Greenwell (1821–1882)

My Vocation

A waif on this earth,
Sick, ugly and small,
Condemned from my birth
And rejected by all,
From my lips broke
"Where – oh where shall I fly?
Who comfort will bring?"
"Sing," said God in reply,
"Chant poor little thing."

Toru Dutt (1856–1877)

Why are you groping like somebody blind

Why are you groping like somebody blind
to find
the Lord?

I advise you, whether you will or no,
to go
within.

He is waiting for you, He is waiting for me,
to see
Him there.

Lalleshwari (1320–1392)

Sometimes they kiss

Sometimes they kiss
when none are near

the sun
and moon.

Why are they shy,
and think it amiss?

We have seen it before.
They have nothing to fear.

Now I have wept three days and more
because He is not with me here:

should not the bride welcome the groom
into her very room?

I have chosen my goods
at Heaven's market –

would that I might have them soon –
the sun and the moon.

The Lord sat in his window one day
as I walked in the sky to pray.

St Catherine of Siena (1347–1380)

False Modesty

How red they go,
the folks whose pants fall down
and leave them all on show.

Such modesty.
The Lord of Life cares not.
It is no novelty.

The world is wide:
the earth His watching eye.
What can you hide?

Akka Mahadevi (c. 1130–1160)

How will you manage

How will you manage to cross the mountains
all alone, and in autumn?
Even when we went the two of us together,
with double the prayers,
it was hard enough.

Princess Ōku (661–702)

Credo

I believe in my heart – a bouquet of scents
that my God bestirs in its leafy rest
to perfume all my life with love
and make it blest.

I believe in my heart – that asks for nothing,
because it holds the dream of all,
the highest dream, the world complete:
my great God's call!

I believe in my heart – that when it sings
it plunges deep in God's hurt side
to rise up from that pool of life
new-magnified.

I believe in my heart – that beats unbid,
and swells the sea with tidal sway
to orchestrate the music of
my joyful day.

I believe in my heart – that I wring to dye
the clothing of my nakedness,
flushed or pale, from which I make
this shining dress.

I believe in my heart – that, timely sown,
took root in the eternal rows,
and, never emptied, gives its harvest
as it grows.

I believe in my heart – that is not gnawed
by worms that dine on earthly death,
but lies in my almighty God
and still has breath.

Gabriela Mistral (1889–1957)

I stopped my travels

I stopped my travels once, to spend some time
amongst the Holy Teachers of the plains.
They said to me: 'Be still. So still that you
can hear your lifeblood flowing through your veins'.

And so I sat in utter quietness
beneath the sky, until I seemed to find
a vaster life within me, and without.
My mind became the world: the world my mind.

Mirabai (1498–c. 1547)

The Best Thing in the World

What's the best thing in the world?
June-rose, by May-dew impearled;
Sweet south-wind, that means no rain;
Truth, not cruel to a friend;
Pleasure, not in haste to end;
Beauty, not self-decked and curled
Till its pride is over-plain;
Love, when, so, you're loved again.
What's the best thing in the world?
Something out of it, I think.

Elizabeth Barrett Browning (1806–1861)

At Lake Balaton

Like a painting of the Flood.
Like inhalations of light.
Like the plains of fairyland.
So secret. So dreamful.
So Heaven-like. So smiling-new.
Balaton when the sky is blue.

Like memories of times lost.
Like the sleep of children.
Like the chiming of the spheres.
So full of thought. So prayerlike.
So peaceful. So far from harm.
Balaton when all is calm.

Like a battle for men's mastery.
Like some doubtful, struggling future.
Like the ragged visions of a fever.
So much at–ache. So full of pain.
So contrary. So hard to please.
Balaton beneath the breeze.

Like a mad ogre.
Like the cries of death.
Like too much hurt.
So fretful. So much in anger.
So tooth-and-nail. So dark aswarm.
Balaton amidst the storm.

Atala Kisfaludy (1836–1911)

A Prayer for Mr T. W.,
Who was then in the West Indies

Thou, whose omniscient eye pervades
Celestial heights, and darkest shades,
Surveys at once each point of land,
And holds the ocean in thy hand,
Preserve this brave advent'rous youth,
And lead him to the paths of truth;
Still o'er his ev'ry thought preside,
And bid his soul in thee confide.
Preserve him, till each danger's o'er,
And land him on his native shore:
Then our exulting heart shall raise
A song of gratitude and praise.

Jane Cave (1754–1812)

In the Forest

Here, O my heart, let us burn the dear dreams that are dead,
Here in this wood let us fashion a funeral pyre
Of fallen white petals and leaves that are mellow and red,
Here let us burn them in noon's flaming torches of fire.

We are weary, my heart, we are weary, so long we have borne
The heavy-loved burden of dreams that are dead, let us rest,
Let us scatter their ashes away, for a while let us mourn;
We will rest, O my heart, till the shadows are grey in the west.

But soon we must rise, O my heart, we must wander again
Into the war of the world and the strife of the throng;
Let us rise, O my heart, let us gather the dreams that remain,
We will conquer the sorrow of life with the sorrow of song.

Sarojini Naidu (1879–1949)

Tell your beads

Tell your beads along the light.
The days soon vanish, one by one.
Who knows when the dark will come.
Time takes all, and soon it's night.

The same old mystery. Who can say?
Don't be a fool, my sister dear:
Tell your beads and hide your face:
We know our Selves are in the way.

Quickly, change your chains for these,
Your beads, and tell them while it's light.
Remake the image of your days.
Make nothing of what once did please.

Follow now the thread, my dear,
Beyond the clattering of the Self.
Tell each drop into the sea.
Where nothing is, is nought to fear.

Gangasati (13th century)

Sonnet

Dear God, if I am truly, by your grace,
A living branch of that all-spreading vine
In whose sweet arms I find my sweetest place
by faith and love – see how I pale and pine.
See how I droop, dear God, and fail and fade.
My leaves grow rank. I wither in their shade.
Come quickly, and my heavy humour mend:
Lighten it to life, dear God, and send
A brighter quickness, so that in Your sight
I drink the dew of Heaven, hour on hour,
And, fed with tears, this withered root may flower.
Be with me, lend me now Your promised light.
I would bear fruit: a harvest sweet that brings
No shame upon the stock from which it springs.

Vittoria Colonna (1492–1547)

Be still, my soul

Be still, my soul: the Lord is on thy side.
Bear patiently the cross of grief or pain.
Leave to thy God to order and provide;
In every change, He faithful will remain.
Be still, my soul: thy best, thy heav'nly Friend
Through thorny ways leads to a joyful end.

Be still, my soul: thy God doth undertake
To guide the future, as He has the past.
Thy hope, thy confidence let nothing shake;
All now mysterious shall be bright at last.
Be still, my soul: the waves and winds still know
His voice Who ruled them while He dwelt below.

Be still, my soul: when dearest friends depart,
And all is darkened in the vale of tears,
Then shalt thou better know His love, His heart,
Who comes to soothe thy sorrow and thy fears.
Be still, my soul: thy Jesus can repay
From His own fullness all He takes away.

Be still, my soul: the hour is hast'ning on
When we shall be forever with the Lord.
When disappointment, grief, and fear are gone,
Sorrow forgot, love's purest joys restored.
Be still, my soul: when change and tears are past
All safe and blessed we shall meet at last.

Be still, my soul: begin the song of praise
On earth, believing, to Thy Lord on high;
Acknowledge Him in all thy words and ways,
So shall He view thee with a well-pleased eye.
Be still, my soul: the Sun of life divine
Through passing clouds shall but more brightly shine.

Catharina Amalia Dorothea von Schlegel (1697–1768)
(translated 1855 by Jane Laurie Borthwick)

Beyond a hundred thousand miles of night

"Beyond a hundred thousand miles of night
behold the gates of Hell", the Angel said.
And there I saw the millions in their pains,
Tearing at their hopeless iron chains.

"Yet still the gates of Hell stand firm: and so
is wickedness confined", the Angel said.
"Pray now in higher hope and better cheer,
That He shall keep thee free from sin and fear."

St Frances of Rome (1384–1440)

Considering the Greatness of Love

I think of Love at every living hour:
Her urgent brightness, and Her stubborn power.
She enters at the gatehouse of my heart,
And thrusts its unresisting doors apart –
And I surrender. Love, I sought delight
in such sweet-solemn battles, day and night.
And so she came and took me prisoner here,
And I am locked in Love, and She is always near.

But am I left in peace? And free from harm?
And is my heart content, my spirit calm?
And do we wander, hand and hand, each day,
each night, the narrow path I thought Love's way?
No, no: for when I tried to rest, or sleep,
within her cell of grace, I could not keep
from Love's fierce, new commands. O happy pain!
O joy! The prisoners of Love do not complain.

There is no knowledge here that may explain
the wonder of this strange subtracting gain:
Her gentle-handed comforts, sweet as wine,
set all my fruits atrembling on the vine:
and yet I beg Her come and gather me,
and use me for Her purpose; take and free
the heart that loves Her; wring it, make it sing,
the trebled hope, the bass of fear in everything.

The truest taste of Love is double-struck:
cruelty and comfort, hurt and luck.
And all the meaning of this Heaven's Hell
wise Solomon himself could never tell.
No sermon can explain the swelling song
that overtops is own bright notes. How long
I fished the pools of Love, how long I tried
each hour – when each already hid its gift inside.

The hook is swinging, and the sea is wide:
but time is short – for we that lie inside
Love's prison shun the things this world can give,
and think on loss, and think on gain, and live
to cling and clamour, counselled by desire,
to clutch this Thing beyond all bliss, this fire,
this song of Love, whose matchless harmony
surpasses all that was, and is, and all that yet may be.

Song of songs, past thought, past every hour
we live: Love singing in its radiant power.
And what cold heart might I persuade with this,
my quiet word? What heart that knows no bliss,
no happy hurt, could I ignite? That does not know
that Love bedecks the warm, the heart aglow,
and suckles it with care upon her breast
and brings it, in its suffering, the sweetest rest.

The strength of Love is past our understanding.
Near or far, it is the same: unending,
and the end of discontent. A peace
that ends all peace: the sweet release
that chains you to its freedom. For it dwells
in Love, and is: remembers and foretells
all life in Loveliness: the placeless place
to rest, for those that gather in Her dear embrace.

Follow Love. Her way is hard and bright.
Let nothing turn you from the happy fight –
not cost, not shame, not fear, not time, not pain,
not any thing. It shall not be in vain.
Obey her terrible commandments. Stay,
and serve her every wish in every way.
Such perfect Lovers come to truth at last,
locked in one another's arms till all this world is passed.

Hadewijch of Brabant (1200–1248)

O God, from Thee we would not stray

O God, from Thee we would not stray:
Reveal to us Thyself, the Way!
Recall us, claim us when we roam!
Thou art our country and our home.

With Thee, in Thee, alone is rest;
Thou art our East, and Thou our West.
Our little lives of thine are part;
No boundaries bar us from thy heart.

Through starless night, through mist and gale,
Thou art the shore toward which we sail;
We bid farewell to friends most kind,
But never leave thy love behind.

And none are alien, none are strange,
Met in the Love that cannot change
We all are brethren in thy Son,
The Father and the children one.

Lucy Larcom (1824–1893)

Dandelions

Welcome children of the Spring,
In your garbs of green and gold,
Lifting up your sun-crowned heads
On the verdant plain and wold.

As a bright and joyous troop
From the breast of earth ye came
Fair and lovely are your cheeks,
With sun-kisses all aflame.

In the dusty streets and lanes,
Where the lowly children play,
There as gentle friends ye smile,
Making brighter life's highway

Dewdrops and the morning sun,
Weave your garments fair and bright,
And we welcome you to-day
As the children of the light.

Children of the earth and sun.
We are slow to understand
All the richness of the gifts
Flowing from our Father's hand.

Were our vision clearer far,
In this sin-dimmed world of ours,
Would we not more thankful be
For the love that sends us flowers?

Welcome, early visitants,
With your sun-crowned golden hair,
With your message to our hearts
Of our Father's loving care.

Frances Ellen Watkins Harper (1825-1911)

I never saw a moor

I never saw a moor,
I never saw the sea,
Yet I know how the heather looks,
And what a wave must be.

I never spoke with God,
Nor visited in Heaven;
Yet certain am I of the spot
As if the chart were given.

Emily Dickinson (1830–1886)

Ever lofty, ever green

Ever lofty, ever green,
rooted surely in the sun,
banners streaming, ever bright,
shining on the round of earth,
what sense or soul can know your light,
what understand your birth.

Ever lofty, ever green,
held tight within the arms of God,
who can know your hidden might,
dazzling as the morning sun,
filled with fire, height on height,
old as time, and new-begun.

Hildegard von Bingen (1098–1179)

A Christian Sonnet

Dear Lord, make peace at last of all my war.
Melt my too-cold heart amidst Your fire.
Let me do one thing in life the more:
Hear you, take Your path, and never tire.
Smother now the passions of my sin.
Cleanse my thoughts of trespass Lord, I pray.
Show my shadow'd eyes Your light within.
Guide me forth to grace, and let me stay.
In You I place my every hope and harm.
My faults are wide: O bring that mercy near
That comes to all who call in sad alarm.
Mend my soul, and keep it, Lord, aright.
Give it wings, and let it fly from here,
Dropping rags of darkness – into light.

Madeleine de l'Aubespine (1546–1596)

World! Why do you hound me so?

World! Why do you hound me so?
Would you distract me from my duty:
Putting beauty in my faith
And not my faith in beauty.

Your silly riches tempt me not
And I would yet a hundredfold
Gather gold unto my love
Than give my love to gold.

A pretty face is soon cast down:
How can I love the loot of time
Or luxury's tin crown?

I look for truth, the greater gain:
To lose the vanities of life –
Not live my life in vain.

Juana Inés de la Cruz (1648–1695)

Beauty's Fragile Light

The seeds give birth; the tender flowers grow.
Too soon the wind and weather lays all low.
They droop and fail and wither unto death
When Summer fades. For Beauty seems a breath,
A season of delight, a coloured hour,
A bright parade without defence or power;
Prey to mortal sickness, age and clime.
There is a Beauty yet beloved of time –
A soul unspotted, holy, pure and clean,
That grows in Heaven's glory, ever-green
In God, unspoiled by Winter's sullen frown,
As sweet as love, and golden as a crown.

Hedvig Charlotta Nordenflycht (1718–1763)

My house was built for two

My house was built for two.
People pass by.
They think I am alone.
But I live with something
that makes the watergrass
and the lily grow,
and the lightning speak in the sky.

Anonymous, Japan (c. 800)

A Christmas Carol, or Verses on the Nativity of Christ

Most blessed time wherein we celebrate,
his happy birth which was both God and man,
Who came to save us from eternal hate,
Such length and depth of mercy none can scan.
We being dead and doomed to live in hell,
by Adams sin of which we all partake:
the promised seed that sentence did expel,
Being given us atonement for to make.
But after such a manner it was done,
as men and Angels could not comprehend,
that our offended God should send his Son
which was true God by death our fault to mend.

Anne Ley (1599–1641)

Sleepsong

Sleep and sleep well, my little one:
but open your eyes
before you sleep,
just for a minute
and look at me.

I want to see the thing,
the thing God gave,
that shines inside
your clear, new eyes
and shines at me.

Now shut your eyes, my little one,
I think I saw
what I wanted to see —
there, everywhere.
Sleep and sleep well now, my little one.

Anonymous, The Gambia

The Pillow

The manger-bed is cold and hard.
I see the Child. He frets and wakes.
He has no pillow for his head.
O friends, my poor heart aches.

Our hearts He wants; our hearts we give;
So we, O friends, are doubly blessed.
Give your heart to be his pillow.
There the Child will rest.

Give it humbly; give it true;
Give it to the Child to keep.
In your tender-gifted hearts
How soft and sure I sleep.

St Thérèse of Lisieux (1873–1897)

Christ, the Nazarene

The copyist group was gathered round
A time-worn fresco, world-renowned,
Whose central glory once had been
The face of Christ, the Nazarene.

And every copyist of the crowd
With his own soul that face endowed,
Gentle, severe, majestic, mean;
But which was Christ, the Nazarene?

Then one who watched them made complaint,
And marvelled, saying, "Wherefore paint
Till ye be sure your eyes have seen
The face of Christ, the Nazarene?"

Constance Naden (1858–1889)

The Crucifixion

A crown of stabbing thorns about your brow,
A wreath of pain, a garland of despite –
And in your eyes the blank despair of night.
I kneel, I bow my head in offering –
And on my shoulders, bright and bittersweet,
The ruby-blood drops from your broken feet.

And none have guessed, and still none know why I,
With troubled looks and ever-darkened brow,
Leave Sunday Mass the last of all; why now
My lips are trembling still, like whispered pain,
While incense lingers in the darkling air
Like pale blue lace, about my evening prayer.

The monks condemn; the sinners burn in Hell –
But in this stone – the Magi gave it me –
The bitter Astarote of love – I see
Thy freedom from the cross, and man's rebirth,
An hour before the sun sets on the earth.

Elisaveta Dmitrieva (1887–1928)

When He died of thirst

When He died of thirst
The water changed to wine.
It happened only once.
There is no second time.

His wine delights no heart.
It dulls no suffering.
It burns like opal-flame.
You gave me fire to drink!

Elisaveta Dmitrieva (1887–1928)

I am a fountain

I am a fountain. You are my water.
I play to You by way of You.

I am an eye. You are my light.
I look for You by way of You.

You are not my right, nor my left.
You are both my feet, and both my arms.

I am a traveller. You are my road.
I come to You by way of You.

Zeynep Hatun (1420–1474)

The Easter Holiday

Through the hush of a Sunday morning a brass fanfare
clangs from the old church tower: God is risen!
He lies no more in his winding-sheets.
And Heaven turns purple above the streets,

and seems to sparkle in flares of gold,
and larks swirl up and sing their songs
like shimmered spots in a violet's eye
and blossoms burst in hope at the sky.

Such revels urge the anxious heart
to start again, and light the sun
and wake the tender, dreaming bud from sleep:

the grave, the Cross, the doubtful hour
are overthrown by Heaven's power.
The bells ring out and, happily, we weep.

Louise Otto-Peters (1819–1895)

Spring Song

Best of all seasons and brightest of all,
Masterpiece-King of the tumbling year,
Painter of light in the newly-cut meadows,
Breath of the broom and the sweet belvedere.

Renewer of trees, of each branch and each bough,
That blazon in loveliest green in the wood:
And the sap of my spirit is stirred, O my God,
And I blossom anew, and resolve to be good.

For whenever the bloom and the leaves renew
Man hopes again, and looks forward with love;
For the grace of God springs forth in his works,
And the strength of our purpose comes from above.

Roses and lilies, and sweet-mottled tulips,
Wave now the banners of Spring to the sky:
And we, in God's sight, and in sweet obligation,
Praise Him amongst them, and ask not why.

Each little bud, each leaf and each meadow
Shows us, as if in a mirror, God's might,
His oneness, His allness, each ever-renewed,
And we read there our hope, and our strength, and our light.

Catharina Regina von Greiffenberg (1633–1694)

Procession of Our Lady of the Ship

She is out, and about!
The little Madonna
Riding her boat.
The world is afloat.
The little Madonna
With a silver crown.
And the four fat oxen are brown
That carry her up on her cart.
Glass pigeons are bringing
Rain from the mountains:
Dead men, dead woman are singing
As they gather by lanes in the misty miles.
O Lady, leave your smile
In the eyes of our cows,
And leave on your long, long gown
The flowers of women dressed for the grave.
And over the brow of Galicia creeps
A dawn that whispers and weeps.
The Madonna looks out on the sea
From the steps of her house.
The world is afloat.
She is out, and about!
The little Madonna
Riding her boat!

Rosalia de Castro (1837–1885)

My life's small ship

My life's small ship sails on alone
Amidst the dark and shades of night:
The waters rage , the wind is high,
I see no shore to left or right.

I know the storm would drown me, Lord,
My sails mischance, my purpose stray,
If You did not watch over me
At every hour, at every day.

And thus upon the restless waves
I go in confidence and calm,
And gaze ahead with childish trust,
Steered from every rock and harm.

You are my light amidst the sea,
Whose depths are less than my deep love:
For You are with me, God, I know,
And guide my course from Heaven above.

I fix my eyes upon the stars,
and though beset with dangers here
I travel with a bright, pure heart,
And know my way, and know no fear.

Such peace amidst the darkling storm,
Such safety still both near and far,
Are Your sweet gifts, and I believe:
You are my Helmsman and my Star.

St Faustina of Poland (1905–1938)

On Death

Tell me Thou safest end of all our woe,
Why wretched mortals do avoid thee so:
Thou gentle drier of th'afflicted tears,
Thou noble ender of the cowards fears;
Thou sweet repose to lovers' sad despair,
Thou calm t'ambitions rough tempestuous care.
If in regard of bliss thou wert a curse,
And then the joys of paradise art worse;
Yet after man from his first station fell,
And God from Eden Adam did expel,
Thou wert no more an evil, but relief;
The balm and cure to ev'ry human grief:
Through thee (what man had forfeited before)
He now enjoys, and ne'er can loose it more.
No subtle serpents in the grave betray,
Worms on the body there, not soul do prey;
No vice there tempts, no terrors there afright,
No coz'ning sin affords a false delight:
No vain contentions do that peace annoy,
No fierce alarms break the lasting Joy.
Such real good as life can never know;
Come when Thou wilt, in thy afrighting'st dress,
Thy shape shall never make thy welcome less.
Thou mayst to joy, but ne'er to fear give birth,
Thou best, as well as certain'st thing on earth.

Fly thee? May travellers then fly their rest,
And hungry infants fly the proffered breast.
No, those that faint and tremble at Thy name,
Fly from their good on a mistaken fame.
Thus childish fear did Israel of old
From plenty and the Promised Land with-hold;
They fancied giants, and refused to go,
When Canaan did with milk and honey flow.

Anne Killigrew (1660–1685)

The Ox

My ox is called
God's-Love.

I feed him
out of my arms

day by day by day.
Dutiful. Undodging.

My ox is called
God's-Love.

I feed him even now
out of my chair,

broken by
his butted thanks,

day by day by day.
Dutiful. Undodging.

Anonymous, Yemen (undated)

Composed During a Thunder-storm

Hark! 'Twas the thunder's awful roar,
That pass'd my ear with solemn sound,
And now the surges dash the shore,
Whilst glaring lightnings stream around.

These horrors now oppress my heart,
I'm filled with dread, with wonder too;
I shrink, and suddenly I start,
As silent this grand scene I view.

But why this start? why this fear?
'Tis causeless sure this wild alarm;
For I will think a *God* is near,
Who still wards off approaching harm.

Judith Lomax (1774–1828)

Prayer for a Sound Sleep

Give me, O Lord, a portion of that rest –
The tranquil calm of Thy repose
On God the Father's all-embracing breast.

Give me, O Lord, a portion of that peace –
The silence of Thy quietude
In Mary's womb, the hush of Thy increase.

I ask this not, O Lord, for my own good –
But that, at each arriving day,
I may be fit to serve Thee as I should.

St Gertrude of Nivelles (626–659)

For Deliverance from a Fever

When sorrows had begirt me round,
And pains within and out,
When in my flesh no part was found,
Then didst Thou rid me out.
My burning flesh in sweat did boil,
My aching head did break,
From side to side for ease I toil,
So faint I could not speak.
Beclouded was my soul with fear
Of Thy displeasure sore,
Nor could I read my evidence
Which oft I read before.
"Hide not Thy face from me!" I cried,
"From burnings keep my soul.
Thou know'st my heart, and hast me tried;
I on Thy mercies roll."
"O heal my soul," Thou know'st I said,
"Though flesh consume to nought,
What though in dust it shall be laid,
To glory 't shall be brought."
Thou heard'st, Thy rod Thou didst remove
And spared my body frail

Thou show'st to me Thy tender love,
My heart no more might quail.
O, praises to my mighty God,
Praise to my Lord, I say,
Who hath redeemed my soul from pit,
Praises to Him for aye.

Anne Bradstreet (1612–1672)

To a Gentleman and Lady on the Death of the Lady's Brother and Sister, and a Child of the Name Avis, Aged One Year

On Death's domain intent I fix my eyes,
Where human nature in vast ruin lies,
With pensive mind I search the drear abode,
Where the great conqu'ror has his spoils bestow'd;
There there the offspring of six thousand years
In endless numbers to my view appears:
Whole kingdoms in his gloomy den are thrust,
And nations mix with their primeval dust:
Insatiate still he gluts the ample tomb;
His is the present, his the age to come
See here a brother, here a sister spread,
And a sweet daughter mingled with the dead.

But, Madam, let your grief be laid aside,
And let the fountain of your tears be dry'd,
In vain they flow to wet the dusty plain,
Your sighs are wafted to the skies in vain,
Your pains they witness, but they can no more,
While Death reigns tyrant o'er this mortal shore.

The glowing stars and silver queen of light
At last must perish in the gloom of night:
Resign thy friends to that Almighty hand,
Which gave them life, and bow to his command;
Thine Avis give without a murm'ring heart,
Though half thy soul be fated to depart.
To shining guards consign thine infant care
To waft triumphant through the seas of air:
Her soul enlarg'd to heav'nly pleasure springs,
She feeds on truth and uncreated things.
Methinks I hear her in the realms above,
And leaning forward with a filial love,
Invite you there to share immortal bliss
Unknown, untasted in a state like this.
With tow'ring hopes, and growing grace arise,
And seek beatitude beyond the skies.

Phillis Wheatley (1753-1784)

Night

The stars are out and shine above.
The eyes of men are shut.
Lovers lie alone with love.
The doors of lords are locked. But

Lord, I am alone with You.

Rabia al-Basri (717-801)

Prayer

O Lord, if I worship You because of Fear of Hell,
    then burn me in Hell;
If I worship You because I desire Paradise,
    then exclude me from Paradise;
But if I worship You for Yourself alone,
    then deny me not your Eternal Beauty.

Rabia al-Basri (717–801)

More than Love

I sit on the lemon verandah
of Heaven
and watch the lights below.

I loved my necklace,
but my neck more.

The ghosts of men and women
shine like oil
in the water of paradise.

I loved my bracelet,
but my wrist more.

Streams of honey
ooze in the basil-grass,
scented with more-than-music.

I loved my ring,
but my finger more.

Love gave me them.
Love gave me this.
Love gave me more than love.

I loved my heart,
but my soul more.

Anonymous, Jordan (16th century)

Indian Love-Song

What are the sins of my race, Beloved,
what are my people to Thee?
And what are Thy shrines, and kine and kindred,
what are Thy gods to me?
Love recks not of feuds and bitter follies,
of stranger, comrade or kin,
Alike in His ear sound the temple bells
and the cry of the muezzin.
For Love shall cancel the ancient wrong
and conquer the ancient rage,
Redeem with His tears the memoried sorrow
that sullied a bygone age.

Sarojini Naidu (1879–1949)

On a Butterfly

Fair, fleet butterfly –
wings of gold and jet –
happy with your hour –
happy to forget –

I watch you as you pass –
gleaming, tumbling, turning –
the coloured breath of Spring –
gone, and yet returning.

Gertrudis Gomez de Alvellaneda (1814–1873)

I am weary now

I am weary now …
Weary now, and long for rest,
The shuttered sleep. O Father blessed,
Let Thy kind and gentle eye
Linger sweetly where I lie,
And if I have sinned today,
Turn Thy patient face away!
Let Jesus' blood and charity
Turn all to good that injures me.
Let my poor spirit understand.
Let all my friends rest in Thy hand.
And let the world be in Thy keeping,
Waking, working, wandering, sleeping:
Comfort, Lord, the sick of soul,
Balm their tears and make them whole.
Set sail the moon across the quiet night:
And watch us, Holy Father, by its light.

Luise Hensel (1798–1876)

Big Wide World

Big wide world,
long and lonely,
stretching on, further than my sight.
And my little feet standing here at its beginning.
I cannot understand its eternity,
its endless cloud of moving dust.
I cannot see behind me. Or what is yet to come.
But You have taken my hand, and my heart;
You have taken my soul – and so
when I think of You,
amidst this world,
I cannot find the end of love.

Veronica Micle (1850–1889)

And when night comes on

And when night comes on
and the dark account makes plain
that all was yet half-done
and much remains to do;
when so many fathoms of shame
and pity are measured out;
then leave all
as it is,
and lay it in the hands of God
and leave the way to Him.
By this, you may come into His peace,
true peace,
and the new day dawning
will be like the light of a new life.

St Edith Stein (1891–1942)

My new white dress

My new white dress,
My yellow morning-blouse,
My tight green wrap,
My hopeful orange shift,
My faded blue singlet,
My big brown gown,
My silver-grey pantaloons,
My torn cream smock,
My cherry party-pants,
My weeding dungarees,
My gorgeous red pyjamas,
My past-it pink T-shirt,
My heavy evening-coat,
My black night-dress,
  God knows
  Death is a thing
  We all have to wear.

Anonymous, Equatorial Guinea (20th century)

The One Certainty

Vanity of vanities, the Preacher saith,
All things are vanity. The eye and ear
Cannot be filled with what they see and hear.
Like early dew, or like the sudden breath
Of wind, or like the grass that withereth,
Is man, tossed to and fro by hope and fear:
So little joy hath he, so little cheer,
Till all things end in the long dust of death.
To-day is still the same as yesterday,
To-morrow also even as one of them;
And there is nothing new under the sun:
Until the ancient race of Time be run,
The old thorns shall grow out of the old stem,
And morning shall be cold and twilight grey.

Christina Rossetti (1830–1894)

Oh, what a lantern

Oh, what a lantern, what a lamp of light
Is thy pure word to me,
To clear my paths and guide my goings right!
I swore and swear again,
I of the statues will observer be,
Thou justly dost ordain.

The heavy weights of grief oppress me sore:
Lord, raise me by the word,
As thou to me didst promise heretofore.
And this unforced praise
I for an off'ring bring, accept, O Lord,
And show to me thy ways.

What if my life lie naked in my hand,
To every chance exposed!
Should I forget what thou dost me command?
No, no, I will not stray
From thy edicts though round about enclosed
With snares the wicked lay.

Thy testimonies as mine heritage,
I have retained still:
And unto them my heart's delight engage,
My heart which still doth bend,
And only bend to do what thou dost will,
And do it to the end.

Mary Sidney Herbert (1561–1621)

Sonnet Written on the Eve of her Execution

Ah, what am I? – and what use is my life?
I am no more than flesh without a heart.
A shadow and a nothing made of pain,
A death in life, a woman torn apart.
Envy me not now, my enemies,
I have no wish for greatness anymore.
Too much sadness clamours round my thoughts.
You do not hurt me as you did before.
And you, my friends still truly fond and dear,
Remember me, who, heartless, lifeless here,
Can do no more of good. Remember me,
Whose life now ends its cruel calamity,
And pray that having suffered here so long,
I may find joy in God's eternity.

Mary Stuart (1542–1587)

The Waiting Pinetree

Have you seen Him yet? The dazzling face
    that lights the way?
I searched for Him, as restless as a stream,
    by night and day.

I stood and called for Him amongst the trees,
    a lonely pine –
my Woodsman with His axe – to wait His heart
    and give Him mine.

I feared His fire, I feared that He would burn
    my limbs away.
But all His flames distilled my soul from substance,
    wine from clay.

Habba Khatoun (1554–1609)

The Volcano Flower

O quiet flower, cast here aside
By Fate, that pleases thus to hide
Your little face upon this waste,
So far from sight, who might be placed
Amidst some happy garden, bright
On some cool terrace, flushed with light,
The pride of some kind master's eye,
Delight of every passer-by –
Alas! unseen by everyone,
You bloom beneath a beating sun,
And those who might esteem your sight
Have other cares besides your plight.
What though you breathe about their feet
Your perfume, petalled, secret-sweet?
And keep, in your extremity,
A drop of honey for the bee?
When men and towns and empires fall,
Who will your little fate recall?
Or search for you, who bore so long,
The mischance of your little wrong?

Amable Tastu (1795–1885)

We Die like Tomorrow

Sad to think that one day,
perhaps tomorrow, all the bright trees
will still be whispering here
and we will not.

And so much sun, dear God, so much
will still be in the world that comes after us:
whole litanies of seasons and rain
that drips quietly from someone's hair ...

The grass grows on
and the moon still hangs amazed
above the wide waters
but we will not come back a second time.

How strange that we can find
in such a little time the time to hate,
when life is just one breath
between the ticks of a clock.

How strange, how sad it is
that we so little look
at the sky, touch grass, and smile —
we who all
so quickly die.

Magda Isanos (1916–1944)

Lullaby

A gold hare squats
on the moon's round reef,
a half-eye open
to watch over you,
so sleep
sleep
sleep.

A bony old man
more wise than all the world,
mashes rice on the moon's round reef
to keep you,
so sleep
sleep
sleep.

Up there is a golden show,
look, on the moon's round reef,
where the soft half-shades
of things in heaven look over you,
so sleep
sleep
sleep.

Evening comes
like red running dye
that someone sends to hush you
so shut your eyes
and sleep
sleep
sleep.

Anonymous, Myanmar (undated)

Morning

Gold and sapphire-tinc't, the day is dawning.
I hurry out along the garden walk
to greet it – gulp the sounds and scents of morning,
the soft-and-sweetly moving air, new-bright,
that flood my heart to overflow with light
so dizzying and bright it might be pain.
My gasping breath gives forth my joy again;
which flies to God in heartfelt thanks for this:
the dazzling resurrection of His bliss.

Maria Brunamonti (1841–1903)

Her Prayer

O Lord my God, be near to me,
as I would wish to be near Thee.
I am Thy sheep. Thou art my Guide.
Let me be always by Thy side.
You know the life that I would live.
It is for Thee alone. Forgive
my sins, and in these trials stand
beside me, Lord, and take my hand.

St Agatha (231–251)

Resignation

Dear God, my Father, King of Kings,
For whom the sun steps out each day,
The bright wind blows, the sweet bird sings,
The waters tumble on their way:

Hear now the soul that worships Thee,
And asks for mercy in distress;
Who, lost in cruel anxiety,
Seeks balm amidst its bitterness.

I only see with saddened eyes
A future dark with midnight pain,
A deathly hurt that never dies.

My worldly sins torment me still:
But if my death-in-life is Thine,
'Fulfil in me, my God, Thy will'.

Brigida Agüero (1837–1866)

At a Graveside

Soon my numbered days will pass,
Like drops into the sea of time;
Soon the empty storm will rave,
And withered grass grow round my grave.

Soon my eyes will fade and close,
The sorrow and the tears be done,
My dust find such a quiet place
As this, amidst the earth's embrace.

Correct me when I doubt my soul;
When thoughts of death unman my heart;
Almighty Father, let me hear
Thy voice of comfort, bright and near,

And when this voice, at death's dark door,
Calls on Thee, then come, I pray,
And take me softly to Thy breast,
And take me gently to my rest.

Anna Maria Lenngren (1754–1817)

Visitors

At my uncle's door,
beside the chicken-run,
I thump the washing
in a tub.

Standing against the wall I see
a cane,
a knobbly staff,
a pair of blue slippers,
a very shiny umbrella,
a pink poncho,
a dusty overcoat,
a bowler-hat,
a beret,
a prudent pair of gumboots,
two purple flipflops,
and a golden scarf …

when I have done thumping,
I go inside,
and there, sitting with Uncle Ndoda,
are eleven souls
having coffee.

Anonymous, Rwanda (19th century)

Psalm

Take time to pray, take time to see;
Seek silence and tranquillity;
And you shall ever be with God the King.
When worlds and peoples come to harm
With battle, clamour and alarm,
He is your stiller peace in everything.

Take time to see, take time to pray,
Before the dust of every day
Lays dark across your mind and dulls the soul.
Seek the face of God on high,
Take time to call the Saviour nigh,
And make your joyful spirit hale and whole.

Take time to pray, take time to see;
Obey the spirit's quiet plea.
When sin would tempt you, still be strong.
And should you fall a moment here,
The Saviour will be always near.
The victory of Sin cannot be long!

Take time to see, take time to pray;
Be rich in grace; seek every day
To look on God, and be like Him the more.
And by His light, more calm and bright,
So you shall come into His sight,
And He to yours, much clearer than before.

Anna Jonassen (1871–1939)

Hymn

Dear God, accept my spring of tears.
I haunt a lightless night of sin.
Be now my Sun, and sweep the clouds
from out the storm I labour in.

Hear, O Lord, my heart's complaint.
Bend Thy ear to my sad song.
God incarnate, at thy feet
I lay my head. I have done wrong.

These feet Eve heard in Paradise
and hid her head in shame and fear.
My sins have left me far from You.
Dear God, have pity, and be near.

I am Thy handmaid. This You know.
Take my hand and make me clean.
I give You mine in shame and hope.
Make this handmaid now Thy queen.

St Kassia of Constantinople (810–865)

Twelve Epigrams

i

Little is plenty
to a grateful heart:
to the ungrateful,
nothing is ever enough.

ii

If you thrive, be generous,
and welcome friends the more:
for such friends will still be with you
should you become poor.

iii

Dear Christ, pray let me be
in careful company
in my adversity:
for this is better than making merry
with fools.

iv

To make a friend in Christ
together
is better than to share
gold and pearls.

v

When two friends both love Christ,
they will thrive by rivalry,
not in the acceptance of equality.

vi

Tears given up for sin
move God more to His mercy.

vii

Talking as you will may rather be
the cause of rudeness:
too much talk, and too much will,
are never good.

viii

All who hate are envious:
envy is begotten in spite.

ix

Wisdom in a fool is mere ornament:
like a bell on a pigsnout.

x

Wealth may buy
some dazzling coverings for sin:
the naked poor
may be seen as they are.

xi

There is no good in poverty,
and there is little in wealth:
the one is the cause of a swollen belly,
the other of a swollen head.

xii

Before you ask for beauty,
Ask for luck: then do your duty.

St Kassia of Constantinople (810–865)

Render alms

Render alms with open hearts.
Keep anger to yourself.
Never cease to learn anew.
Value what is true.

Persevere in all good things.
Speak no unkind word.
Pray for knowledge and for light.
Value what is right.

Never lie or carry tales.
Give to those who need.
Do as holy people would.
Value what is good.

Avvaiyar (c. 3rd Century BC)

Index of first lines

A crown of stabbing thorns about your brow	30
A gold hare squats	57
A waif on this earth	3
Ah, what am I? – and what use is my life?	53
All who hate are envious	65
And when night comes on	49
At my uncle's door	61
Be still, my soul: the Lord is on thy side	14
Before you as for beauty	65
Best of all seasons and brightest of all	33
Beyond a hundred thousand miles of night	15
Big wide world	48
Dear Christ, pray let me be	64
Dear God, accept my spring of tears	63
Dear God, if I am truly, by your grace	13
Dear God, my Father, King of Kings	59
Dear Lord, make peace at last of all my war	23
Ever lofty, ever green	22
Fair, fleet butterfly	46
Give me, O Lord, a portion of that rest	40
Gold and sapphire-tinc't, the day is dawning	58
Hark! Twas the thunder's awful roar	39
Have you seen Him yet? The dazzling face	54
Here, O my heart, let us burn the dear dreams that are dead	11
How red they go	5
How will you manage to cross the mountains	5
I am a fountain. You are my water	31
I am not skilled to understand	2
I am weary now	47
I believe in my heart – a bouquet of scents	6

I never saw a moor	21
I sit on the lemon verandah	45
I stopped my travels once, to spend some time	7
I think of Love at every living hour	16
If you thrive, be generous	64
Like a painting of the Flood	9
Little is plenty	64
Most blessed time wherein we celebrate	26
My house was built for two	25
My life's small ship sails on alone	35
My new white dress	50
My ox is called God's-Love	38
O God, from Thee we would not stray	19
O Lord my God, be near to me	58
O Lord, if I worship You because of Fear of Hell	44
O quiet flower, cast here aside	55
Oh, what a lantern, what a lamp of light	52
On Death's domain intent I fix my eyes	42
Render alms with open hearts	66
Sad to think that one day	56
She is out, and about!	34
Sleep and sleep well, my little one	27
Sometimes they kiss	4
Soon my numbered days will pass	60
Take time to pray, take time to see	62
Talking as you will may rather be	65
Tears given up for sin	65
Tell me Thou safest end of all our woe	36
Tell your beads along the light	12
The copyist group was gathered round	29
The manger-bed is cold and hard	28
The seeds give birth; the tender flowers grow	25
The stars are out and shine above	44

There is no good in poverty 65

Thou, whose omniscient eye pervades 10

Through the hush of a Sunday morning a brass fanfare 32

To make a friend in Christ 64

Two little words from Him were enough 1

Vanity of vanities, the Preacher saith 51

Wealth may buy 65

Welcome children of the Spring 20

What are the sins of my race, Beloved 46

What's the best thing in the world? 8

When He died of thirst 31

When sorrows had begirt me round 41

When two friends both love Christ, 64

Why are you groping like somebody blind 3

Wisdom in a fool is mere ornament 65

World! Why do you hound me so? 24

Index of Authors

St Agatha	58
Brigida Agüero	59
Madeleine de l'Aubespine	23
Avvaiyar	66
Anne Bradstreet	41
Elizabeth Barrett Browning	8
Maria Brunamonti	58
Rosalia de Castro	34
St Catherine of Siena	4
Jane Cave	10
Vittoria Colonna	13
Juana Inés de la Cruz	24
Emily Dickinson	21
Elisaveta Dmitrieva	30–1
Toru Dutt	3
Anonymous, Equatorial Guinea	50
St Faustina of Poland	35
St Frances of Rome	15
Anonymous, The Gambia	27
Gangasati	12
St Gertrude of Nivelles	40
Gertrudis Gomez de Alvellaneda	46
Dora Greenwell	2
Catharina Regina von Greiffenberg	33
Hadewijch of Brabant	16–18
Frances Ellen Watkins Harper	20–1
Zeynep Hatun	31
Luise Hensel	47
Mary Sidney Herbert	52
Hildegard von Bingen	22
Magda Isanos	56

Anonymous, Japan   25

Anna Jonassen   62

Anonymous, Jordan   45

St Kassia of Constantinople   63–5

Habba Khatoun   54

Anne Killigrew   36–7

Atala Kisfaludy   9

Lalleshwari   3

Lucy Larcom   19

Anna Maria Lenngren   60

Anne Ley   26

Judith Lomax   39

Akka Mahadevi   5

Veronica Micle   48

Mirabai   7

Gabriela Mistral   6–7

Anonymous, Myanmar   57

Constance Naden   29

Sarojini Naidu   11, 46

Hedvig Charlotta Nordenflycht   25

Princess Ōku   5

Louise Otto-Peters   32

Rabia al-Basri   44

Christina Rossetti   51

Anonymous, Rwanda   61

Catharina Amalia Dorothea von Schlegel   14–15

St Edith Stein   49

Mary Stuart   53

Amable Tastu   55

St Teresa of Ávila   1

St Thérèse of Lisieux   28

Phillis Wheatley   42–3

Anonymous, Yemen   38

SLG PRESS PUBLICATIONS

FP1   *Prayer and the Life of Reconciliation*   Gilbert Shaw (1969)
FP2   *Aloneness Not Loneliness*   Mother Mary Clare SLG (1969)
FP4   *Intercession*   Mother Mary Clare SLG (1969)
FP8   *Prayer: Extracts from the Teaching of Fr Gilbert Shaw*   Gilbert Shaw (1973)
FP12 *Learning to Pray*   Mother Mary Clare SLG (1970)
FP15 *Death, the Gateway to Life*   Gilbert Shaw (1971)
FP16 *The Victory of the Cross*   Dumitru Stăniloae (1970)
FP26 *The Message of Saint Seraphim*   Irina Gorainov (1974)
FP28 *Julian of Norwich: Four Studies to Commemorate the Sixth Centenary
      of the Revelations of Divine Love*   Sr Benedicta Ward SLG,
                                  Sr Eileen Mary SLG, ed. A. M. Allchin (1973)
FP43 *The Power of the Name: The Jesus Prayer in Orthodox Spirituality* Kallistos Ware (1974)
FP46 *Prayer and Contemplation* and *Distractions are for Healing*   Robert Llewelyn (1975)
FP48 *The Wisdom of the Desert Fathers*   trans. Sr Benedicta Ward SLG (1975)
FP50 *Letters of Saint Antony the Great*   trans. Derwas Chitty (1975, 2nd edn 2021)
FP54 *From Loneliness to Solitude*   Roland Walls (1976)
FP55 *Theology and Spirituality*   Andrew Louth (1976, rev. 1978)
FP61 *Kabir: The Way of Love and Paradox*   Sr Rosemary SLG (1977)
FP62 *Anselm of Canterbury: A Monastic Scholar*   Sr Benedicta Ward SLG (1973)
FP63 *Evelyn Underhill, Anglican Mystic: Two Centenary Essays*
                            A. M. Allchin, Bp Michael Ramsey (2nd edn 1996)
FP67 *Mary and the Mystery of the Incarnation: An Essay on the Mother of God
      in the Theology of Karl Barth*   Andrew Louth (1977)
FP68 *Trinity and Incarnation in Anglican Tradition*   A. M. Allchin (1977)
FP70 *Facing Depression*   Gonville ffrench-Beytagh (1978, 2nd edn 2020)
FP71 *The Single Person*   Philip Welsh (1979)
FP72 *The Letters of Ammonas, Successor of St Antony*   trans. Derwas Chitty (1979)
FP74 *George Herbert, Priest and Poet*   Kenneth Mason (1980)
FP75 *A Study of Wisdom: Three Tracts by the Author of* The Cloud of Unknowing
                                          trans. Clifton Wolters (1980)
FP78 *Silence in Prayer and Action*   Sr Edmée SLG (1981)
FP81 *The Psalms: Prayer Book of the Bible*   Dietrich Bonhoeffer, trans. Sr Isabel SLG (1982)
FP82 *Prayer and Holiness*   Dumitru Stăniloae (1982)
FP85 *Walter Hilton: Eight Chapters on Perfection and Angels' Song*
                                          trans. Rosemary Dorward (1983)
FP88 *Creative Suffering*   Iulia de Beausobre (1989)
FP90 *Bringing Forth Christ: Five Feasts of the Child Jesus by St Bonaventure*
                                          trans. Eric Doyle OFM (1984)
FP92 *Gentleness in John of the Cross*   Thomas Kane (1985)
FP93 *Prayer: The Work of the Spirit*   Sr Edmée SLG (1985)
FP94 *Saint Gregory Nazianzen: Selected Poems*   trans. John McGuckin (1986)

FP95   *The World of the Desert Fathers: Stories & Sayings from the Anonymous Series of the 'Apophthegmata Patrum'*   trans. Columba Stewart OSB (1986, 2nd edn 2020)

FP101   *Anglicanism: A Canterbury Essay*   Kenneth Mason (1987)

FP104   *Growing Old with God*   T. N. Rudd (1988, 2nd edn 2020)

FP105   *The Simplicity of Prayer: Extracts from the Teaching of Mother Mary Clare SLG*   Mother Mary Clare SLG (1988)

FP106   *Julian Reconsidered*   Kenneth Leech, Sr Benedicta SLG (1988)

FP108   *The Unicorn: Meditations on the Love of God*   Harry Galbraith Miller (1989)

FP109   *The Creativity of Diminishment*   Sister Anke (1990)

FP111   *A Kind of Watershed: An Anglican Lay View of Sacramental Confession*   Christine North (1990)

FP116   *Jesus, the Living Lord*   Bp Michael Ramsey (1992)

FP117   *The Spirituality of Saint Cuthbert*   Sr Benedicta Ward SLG (1992)

FP120   *The Monastic Letters of St Athanasius the Great*   trans. Leslie Barnard (1994)

FP122   *The Hidden Joy*   Sr Jane SLG, ed. Dorothy Sutherland (1994)

FP123   *At the Lighting of the Lamps: Hymns of the Ancient Church*   trans. John McGuckin (1995)

FP124   *Prayer of the Heart: An Approach to Silent Prayer and Prayer in the Night*   Alexander Ryrie (1995, 3rd edn 2020)

FP125   *Whole Christ: The Spirituality of Ministry*   Philip Seddon (1996)

FP127   *Apostolate and the Mirrors of Paradox*   Sydney Evans, ed. Andrew Linzey, Brian Horne (1996)

FP128   *The Wisdom of Saint Isaac the Syrian*   Sebastian Brock (1997)

FP129   *Saint Thérèse of Lisieux: Her Relevance for Today*   Sr Eileen Mary SLG (1997)

FP130   *Expectations: Five Addresses for Those Beginning Ministry*   Sr Edmée SLG (1997)

FP131   *Scenes from Animal Life: Fables for the Enneagram Types*   Waltraud Kirschke, trans. Sr Isabel SLG (1998)

FP132   *Praying the Word of God: The Use of Lectio Divina*   Charles Dumont OCSO (1999)

FP134   *The Hidden Way of Love: Jean-Pierre de Caussade's Spirituality of Abandonment*   Barry Conaway (1999)

FP135   *Shepherd and Servant: The Spiritual Theology of Saint Dunstan*   Douglas Dales (2000)

FP136   *Eternity and Time*   Dumitru Stăniloae, trans. A. M. Allchin (2001)

FP137   *Pilgrimage of the Heart*   Sr Benedicta Ward SLG (2001)

FP138   *Mixed Life*   Walter Hilton, trans. Rosemary Dorward (2001)

FP140   *A Great Joy: Reflections on the Meaning of Christmas*   Kenneth Mason (2001)

FP141   *Bede and the Psalter*   Sr Benedicta Ward SLG (2002)

FP142   *Abhishiktananda: A Memoir of Dom Henri Le Saux*   Murray Rogers, David Barton (2003)

FP143   *Friendship in God: The Encounter of Evelyn Underhill & Sorella Maria of Campello*   A. M. Allchin (2003)

FP144   *Christian Imagination in Poetry and Polity: Some Anglican Voices from Temple to Herbert*   Archbp Rowan Williams (2004)

FP145   *The Reflections of Abba Zosimas, Monk of the Palestinian Desert*   trans. John Chryssavgis (2004)

FP146   *The Gift of Theology: The Trinitarian Vision of Ann Griffiths and Elizabeth of Dijon*   A. M. Allchin (2005)

FP147 *Sacrifice and Spirit*   Bp Michael Ramsey (2005)
FP148 *Saint John Cassian on Prayer*   trans. A. M Casiday (2006)
FP149 *Hymns of Saint Ephrem the Syrian*   trans. Mary Hansbury (2006)
FP150 *Suffering: Why all this suffering? What Do I Do about it?*
                                  Reinhard Körner OCD, trans. Sr Avis Mary SLG (2006)
FP151 *A True Easter: The Synod of Whitby 664 AD*   Sr Benedicta Ward SLG (2007)
FP152 *Prayer as Self-Offering*   Alexander Ryrie (2007)
FP153 *From Perfection to the Elixir: How George Herbert Fashioned a Famous Poem*
                                                 Ben de la Mare (2008)
FP154 *The Jesus Prayer: Gospel Soundings*   Sr Pauline Margaret CHN (2008)
FP155 *Loving God Whatever: Through the Year with Sister Jane*   Sister Jane SLG (2006)
FP156 *Prayer and Meditation for a Sleepless Night*
                                      SISTERS OF THE LOVE OF GOD (2nd edn 2009)
FP157 *Being There: Caring for the Bereaved*   John Porter (2009)
FP158 *Learn to Be at Peace: The Practice of Stillness*   Andrew Norman (2010)
FP159 *From Holy Week to Easter*   George Pattison (2010)
FP160 *Strength in Weakness: The Scandal of the Cross*   John W. Rogerson (2010)
FP161 *Augustine Baker: Frontiers of the Spirit*   Victor de Waal (2010)
FP162 *Out of the Depths*
                  Gonville ffrench-Beytagh; epilogue Wendy Robinson (2nd edn 2010)
FP163 *God and Darkness: A Carmelite Perspective*
                            Gemma Hinricher OCD, trans. Sr Avis Mary SLG (2010)
FP164 *The Gift of Joy*   Curtis Almquist SSJE (2011)
FP165 *'I Have Called You Friends': Suggestions for the Spiritual Life Based on*
     the Farewell Discourses of Jesus   Reinhard Körner OCD (2012)
FP166 *Leisure*   Mother Mary Clare SLG (2012)
FP167 *Carmelite Ascent: An Introduction to St Teresa and St John of the Cross*
                                Mother Mary Clare SLG (rev. edn 2012)
FP168 *Ann Griffiths and her Writings*   Llewellyn Cumings (2012)
FP169 *The Our Father*   Sr Benedicta Ward SLG (2012)
FP170 *Exploring Silence*   Wendy Robinson (1974, 3rd edn 2013)
FP171 *The Spiritual Wisdom of the Syriac Book of Steps*   Robert A Kitchen (2013)
FP172 *The Prayer of Silence*   Alexander Ryrie (2012)
FP173 *On Tour in Byzantium: Excerpts from The Spiritual Meadow of John Moschus*
                                     Ralph Martin SSM (2013)
FP174 *Monastic Life*   Bonnie Thurston (2016)
FP175 *Shall All Be Well? Reflections for Holy Week*   Graham Ward (2015)
FP176 *Solitude and Communion: Papers on the Hermit Life*   ed. A. M. Allchin (2015)
FP177 *The Prayers of Jacob of Serugh*   ed. Mary Hansbury (2015)
FP178 *The Monastic Hours of Prayer*   Sr Benedicta Ward SLG (2016)
FP179 *The Desert of the Heart: Daily Readings with the Desert Fathers*
                                  trans. Sr Benedicta Ward SLG (2016)
FP180 *In Company with Christ: Lent, Palm Sunday, Good Friday & Easter to Pentecost*
                                  Sr Benedicta Ward SLG (2016)
FP181 *Lazarus: Come Out! Reflections on John 11*   Bonnie Thurston (2017)

FP182 *Unknowing & Astonishment: Meditations on Faith for the Long Haul*
Christopher Scott (2018)

FP183 *Pondering, Praying, Preaching: Romans 8*   Bonnie Thurston (2nd edn 2021)

FP184 *Shem'on the Graceful: Discourse on the Solitary Life*
trans. with introd. Mary Hansbury (2020)

FP185 *God Under my Roof: Celtic Songs and Blessings (revised and enlarged edition)*
Esther de Waal (2020)

FP186 *Journeying with the Jesus Prayer*   James F. Wellington (2020)

FP187 *Poet of the Word: Re-reading Scripture with Ephraem the Syrian*
Aelred Partridge OC (2020)

FP188 *Identity and Ritual*   Alan Griffiths (2021)

FP189 *River of the Spirit: The Spirituality of Simon Barrington-Ward*   Andy Lord (2021)

FP190 *Prayer and the Struggle Against Evil*   John Barton, Daniel Lloyd,
James Ramsay, Alexander Ryrie (2021)

FP191 *Dante's Spiritual Journey: A Reading of the Divine Comedy*   Tony Dickinson (2021)

FP192 *Jesus the Undistorted Image of God*   John Townroe (2022)

FP193 *Our Deepest Desire: Prayer, Fasting & Almsgiving in the Writings of*
St Augustine of Hippo   Sr Susan SLG (2022)

FP194 *Lent with George Herbert*   Tony Dickinson (2022)

FP195 *Four Ways to the Cross*   Tony Dickinson (2022)

FP200 *Monastic Vocation*   Sisters of the Love of God, Abp Rowan Williams (2021)

CONTEMPLATIVE POETRY SERIES

CP1 *Amado Nervo: Poems of Faith and Doubt*   trans. John Gallas (2021)

CP2 *Anglo-Saxon Poets: The High Roof of Heaven*   trans. John Gallas (2021)

CP3 *Middle English Poets: Where Grace Grows Ever Green*   trans. & ed. John Gallas (2021)

CP4 *Selected Poems: The Voice Inside our Home*   Edward Clarke (2022)

CP5 *Women & God: Drops in the Sea of Time*   trans. & ed. John Gallas (2022)

VESTRY GUIDES

VG1 *The Visiting Minister: How to Welcome Visiting Clergy to your Church* Paul Monk (2021)

VG2 *Help! No Minister! or Please Take the Service*   Paul Monk (2022)

slgpress.co.uk